100 WRITINGS FOR A MODERN WORLD VOLUME I

Ken G. Jackson

A variety of poems about social issues, politics, love, and the state of living in today's world; at times satirical, ironic, humorous, and sad.

KGJ Publishing
Copyright © 2018 by Kenneth G. Jackson

gjaxnek@gmail.com

All rights reserved. Published in the United States by KGJ Publishing, Elmhurst, IL.

ISBN: 978-0-692-13747-5

Printed in the United States by Publisher's Graphics®, Carol Stream, IL

CONTENTS

POEMS

1. I REMEMBER HOW HE PRAYED (DAD'S PASSING) p.1
2. "A PICTURE'S WORTH A THOUSAND WORDS" p.3
3. ARE THE FOREIGNER'S NEXT TO ME p.4
4. CASHING IN ON JESUS p.5
5. COLLECTED IN BROKEN DOWN CORN CRIBS p.7
6. CONCERNS p.8
7. GROWN UP MEN p.9
8. CONTEMPLATE THE KITCHEN p.11
9. MY ULTRA-PEACE p.12
10. COSMETIC SURGERY p.14
11. LIFE IS EASY p.15
12. DO I KNOW THAT GUY? p.17
13. FEEL THE COLD p.18
14. GRANULES OF SALT p.19
15. MY DREAMSCAPE p.20
16. EARTHLINGS PARADOX p.21
17. HER CURLS CIRCLE HER HEAD p.22
18. HER EFFERVESCENT BEAUTY p.23
19. MINORITIES ON THE BUS p.24
20. I FOUND A SHELTERED GARDEN p.25
21. I AM A NOBODY TO YOU p.27
22. DID I READ A BOOK AGAIN? p.28
23. IT'S COMPLICATED p.29
24. I AM JUST THE NAKED QUARRY p.30
25. I SAW A LITTLE BABY p.31

26. THE GAY WEDDING   p.32
27. I'M JUST HERE TO LOOK GOOD   p.34
28. I BUY WHAT I WANT (THE MIRACLE
MAN)   p.36
29. A GOOD WALKING ROAD   p.37
30. I CANNOT   p.38
31. HE HAD LOST ONE ARM   p.39
32. I HAVE BREATHED MY FINAL BREATH
p.40
33. HERE COMES THAT HYBRID BUS p.41
34. WANING MOON   p.42
35. UNKNOWN UNKNOWNS   p.43
36. I REMEMBER   p.44
37. I SMELL THE GRASS IN THE
YARD   p.45
38. IT'S ONLY A SONG   p.46
39. I KNOW I LOVE THE RAIN   p.48
40. I WALKED THE LAKE TODAY   p.49
41. THE CAT WON'T SPEAK TO ME   p.50
42. OVERHEARING THE BIOLOGICAL
PARENTS   p.51
43. IF ONE MORE GIRL SAYS NO   p.52
44. IF THE HAPPINESS OF OTHERS   p.53
45. I'M GOING TO SCHOOL TODAY   p.54
46. MY DOG IS SILLY   p.55
47. I WAS A NOBODY   p.56
48. I'M JUST HERE AMONG YOU   p.58
49.I'M WATCHING YOUNG PEOPLE   p.60
50. I'M WEARING A PEACE SHIRT   p.61
51. INDIFFERENCE REMARKABLE   p.63
52. "NOW I LAY ME DOWN TO
SLEEP" NO. 2   p.64

53. MY BACKSIDE   p.66
54. KILL A TERRORIST   p.67
55. LIBERAL GUILT   p.68
56. MEMORIAL DAY   p.69
57. RACISM IN THE BAR   p.71
58. I WILL KILL THAT THING   p.73
59. PUT ME IN A ROOM   p.74
60. SAGGING PORCH   p.75
61. SEE THE YOUNG TEENS   p.76
62. SEEMS A TIME THAT WAS
BLESSED   p.77
63. SHE'S ALL GROWN UP   p.78
64. TALK, TALK   p.79
65. THAT AMAZING BODY   p.80
66. I WATCHED THE BAND
CAREFULLY   p.83
67. THE LITTLE GIRLS   p.84
68. YOU BOYS USED TO LIE ON THE
GROUND   p.85
69. THE MOON SHONE LIKE A SILVER
PLATE   p.88
70. THE NEWS WAS DISMAL   p.89
71. THERE'S A BMW   p.91
72. THE SUN SHONE   p.93
73. THE CHICAGO HOMELESS MONITORS
p.94
74. THE URBAN BOISTROUS BOY   p.96
75. I'M DIGGING OUT THE COAL   p.97
76. A NEW SOFT WIND   p.99
77. THERE'S AN OLD MAN   p.100
78. THERE'S ANOTHER CONDO   p.101

79. THERE'S SOMETHING COMING FROM YOUR EAR   p.102

80. TIME IS FAR AWAY   p.104

81. VICTIM OF YOUTH CULTURE   p.106

82. WONDERING   p.108

83. YOU HAVE ALL THE MONEY   p.109

84. MODERN WIFE   p.111

85. HELLO THERE, PEOPLE   p.112

86. I'D LIKE TO BE A HOUSEWIFE   p.114

87. BREATHE IN THE AIR   p.115

88. LITTLE LIBRARY PENCILS   p.117

89. THE FLOWERS ARE YET TO BLOSSOM   p.118

90. TEARS WASH THIS SOUL SO CLEAN   p.119

91. THE PLEASURE DOME   p.120

92. OBAMA   CHICAGO   2008   p.122

93. MAYBE MAYBERRY   p.123

94. I KNELT TODAY AT THE FOOTBALL GAME   p.125

95. THE CONFIRMATION   p.126

96. A FUTURE LEGISLATIVE LAW   p.128

97. CHASE THE DEMON   p.129

98. MY MIND IS BLANK   p.134

99. HAPPINESS   p.135

100. TO THIS BLESSING I WILL COME (MOM'S PASSING)   p.136

To Ian and Eric

"The More Things Change, The More They
Stay the Same."
- Popular Proverb and True -

WIKIPEDIA: A proverb of French origin, used by
the French novelist Alphonse Karr (1808-90);
"Random House Dictionary of Popular Proverbs and
Sayings" by Gregory Y. Titelman (Random House,
New York, 1996).

<u>1</u>

I Remember How He Prayed (Dad's Passing)

I remember how he prayed
With an eloquence that flowed with ease,
As we gathered round the table
On those special days.
I see him talking about his family
And watch the joy or ache emerge in his eye.
I feel him in the field,
Surveying the land and exulting in its beauty.
I see him late at night,
Speaking of the grief in the world
And asking for some answers.
I watch him gliding effortlessly across the lake,
Skates glinting off the ice,
Joy radiating from his ruddy face.
I see him smiling warmly,
Enjoying the company of others,
Sitting with my mother,
Teasing her just a bit
With soft and subtle manner.
I feel the love envelop his grandchildren
As he swings them high over his head,
And they giggle with glee.

I watch his eyes moisten,
Emotions stirring deep within
When his feelings were touched.
He walked with proud simplicity
Among his family and friends,
Leaving his mark in untold ways.
A gentler man we never knew,
Who always tried and cared and listened
Through joy or despair.
His memory remains firmly
Implanted in our minds,
To hold near and dear,
A gift to be recalled on quiet evenings,
To inspire us with his example,
To know the goodness capable of men.
"Blessed are the peacemakers…for they shall
inherit the earth. (Matt. 5:9 and 5:5)."

2

"A Picture's Worth a Thousand Words"

"A picture's worth a thousand words,"
A picture is so phony,
That smile that spreads behind your lips,
Hides all that is so lonely.

<u>3</u>

Are the Foreigner's Next to Me?

Are the foreigner's next to me
on vacation,
Or perhaps contributing members
of this Great Nation?

They are speaking European
and look much like me.
The woman's quite attractive.
They both are very clean,
and reading all those books
about hygiene.

In here are no Latino's
with soiled hands and shirts,
left standing by a pickup truck,
wait all day for work.

<u>4</u>

Cashing in on jesus

Cashing in on jesus,
The All-American way,
It's become the latest lifestyle,
Not just asking if you're saved.

Your own, personal jesus,
Created every day,
Built to suit your fancy,
You don't even have to pray.

Just read a book or two,
An expert you'll become,
I'm not talking 'bout the Bible,
Not all passages are fun.

Or catch yourself a movie,
His life you will behold,
And feel the things that jesus felt,
All broad and big and sold.

You can talk and talk and wonder,
While watching your TV,
And pretty soon discover,
Just what you do believe.

If you fail, keep trying,
I'm sure you'll find that link,
Cuz there's a jesus just for you,
And everything you think.

5

Collected in Broken Down Corn Cribs

Collected in broken-down cribs,
Corn dribbles on the ground,
Feeding the critters,
Scurrying through the shadows,
Moonlight spreading over
The bleeding corn rows.

Gray, ramshackle houses close by,
Beaten by the sun,
Needing more than painting long ago,
Scatter across the flatlands,
Pleading for mercy.

6

Concerns

Concerns
about the starving children,
Images of bloated bellies
and flies.
If they were European,
not African,
We would be rushing
to their sides,
Not watching late night ads,
pleading for breadcrumbs.

<u>7</u>

Grown Up Men

Grown up men
speak in firm overtones to other men
and interrupt and know
they know more
and if they speak loudly
they'll be more right.

Grown up men
put down other men
to carve out their place
to leave others dangling
weak with unease.

Grown up men
feign listening to wise, lovely
women
or mother-like substitutes
and give sway or ignore
or barter sexuality
in hidden overtures
and smile courageously
to get their way
in flirtatious moments.

Grown up men and women
of power
gather in boardrooms
and gloat over the same things
and laugh at the same things
and celebrate themselves
with the same toasts
and have become the same.
None the fairer of the sexes.

<u>8</u>

Contemplate the Kitchen

Contemplate the kitchen
Knives and spoons and forks
Cabinets that glisten
Counters that evoke
A sense of well-being
All's right with the world
Everything is in its place
As pretty as a pearl.
How I love my kitchen
All bright and clean and white
Of course, we never eat here
It would wreck this lovely sight.

9

My Ultra-Peace

Now and then
I stop and think
a bit about
my ultra-peace
The times I go
deep within
and forget about
where I've been
or right or wrong
or weak or strong
or lines and lines
of teeming throngs
heads bowed down
to their phones
bustling busy
to and fro
wonder where they have to go
awful fast
move their feet
pounding on the broken street.
Silence they have never seen
felt or smelled
or stirred beneath
That grinding sound

they must make
lack of motion
their earthquake
Perhaps cynical I've become
To navel starring I've succumbed.

10

Cosmetic Surgery

Cosmetic Surgery
Come right in
Change your face
On a whim.

Do your thing
Make it big
Or even smaller
If that's what you wish.

And when you're done
They'll (you'll) like you more
Hope you're better
Then you were before.

But who's to know?
Who's to tell?
Your body's just
Your wishing well.

<u>11</u>

Life Is Easy

Life is easy,
all a pool of water
to slip into, soothing,
on a hot day.

Life is easy,
handed to me on
a silver platter,
yet I spill, sometimes,
and the tea ends up in the
beige carpet, staining.
I just move on.

"Life is easy,
get on with it,"
He said
from the luxury apartment,
another skyscraper
looming across the window view.

Life is easy
for those who don't want.
Dropped a silver dollar down
the grate and forgot
about it.

-15-

But that silver dollar
for the others
is not forgotten.
Perhaps gum on the bottom
of the homeless man's cane can
retrieve it.

But that isn't easy.

12

Do I Know That Guy?

Do I know that guy?
He seemed to think so.
Very loud and friendly.
Shook my hand quite firmly.
Exalting in baseball.
Crunching peanuts and popcorn.
Drinking large amounts of liquor.
Very happy with himself.
Do I know that guy?

<u>13</u>

Feel the Cold

Feel the cold
Coming to attention
On frosty morns
As the last man falls out
And the child shivers alone
In bombed-out buildings.

<u>14</u>

Granules of Salt

Granules of salt
Dried perspiration
Lie on my brow
Seasoning my life
But too much
Enters my eyes
And stings until I
Can no longer see.

<u>15</u>

My Dreamscape

My dreamscape is a seascape,
Turtles swimming by,
Seashells in their pockets,
Wishing they could fly.

Sharks, they are finless,
Danger lurks below,
But we never see them,
Because the fins don't show.

Octopuses matter,
Tentacles intrude,
Hug the nearby diver,
Always tried and true,

The clownfish, he's a soldier,
Wears his orange and black,
Won't salute the major,
And never will attack,

And me, a barracuda,
Clinging to that boat,
Drifting off to paradise,
Feeling so much hope.

<u>16</u>

Earthling Paradox

Diligently looking for life elsewhere,
While absently killing it here.

17

Her Curls Circle Her Head

Her curls circle her head,
like a crown,
her crown,
but my crown
of love,
I see every morning,
barely breaking the covers,
cascading over the pillow,
soon to reveal that smile
so fresh,
so fresh to me,
that delicate
reservoir of love,
you are,
you always will be
in my heart,
My heart so now
full of you.

<u>18</u>

Her Effervescent Beauty

Her effervescent beauty
touches me,
only visually,
But I feel her smile
inside,
And warm, and grow,
and think I know,
She could become
the One,
Forgetting,
this is the same thing
My mind has done
before,
wanting more
than reality likely has in
store.

Breaking my heart
when what's never
started
is over.

19

Minorities on the Bus

Minorities on the bus,
Mingled all together,
Mercedes goes flying by,
Holds that white fella.

<u>20</u>

I Found a Sheltered Garden

I found a sheltered garden,
where light danced upon little leaves,
the crackling vines,
still nearly winter barren,
crawled along the wall,
and wispy branches spread from the
diminutive trees,
which stood alongside the rough-hewn,
but welcoming bench;
sprinkled about were rebirthing grasses,
yellow flowers knelt
in the burgeoning bed,
surrounded by the light,
illuminating the array of shrubbery,
like droplets of dew
reflected this wondrous day
right back to me and you.

(the nearby evergreen stood,
mother-like,
limbs stretched forth,
somewhat sagging from former snows,
now waited,

like the others,
for the full sheath of spring's rays,
to lift those weary arms skyward)

21

I Am a Nobody to You

I am a nobody to you
I matter nothing to you
I am a figure passing in the night
for you.

You are successful
You have achieved
You are leisurely living
Overlooking the lake
Exclaiming of the perfect
Early morning sun
Sprinkling in your sitting room.

Maybe I was an interesting face
Maybe I was a momentary lapse
Maybe I was a fanciful dance
An alcohol-fueled extravagance
A parlor room of games
Not flesh and blood
Full of feelings
Now hurt
And bewildered
by your retreat.

22

Did I Read a Book Again?

Did I read a book again?
If so I don't remember when.
Lying on my bedroom floor,
Gathered there they look so bored.
Should I take the time and pain
To pick one up and feed my brain
When I can gain what I must get
By leaving on my TV set.

23

It's Complicated

Too bad I was aborted
before I had my say
before I could become
the man I am today.

<u>24</u>

I Am Just the Naked Quarry

I am just the naked quarry,
In the savage hunter's sights,
Bounding through the long, lost glories,
Trees replaced by high-rise lights.

Camouflaged against the buildings,
Window glass reflects so real,
Only see me when I'm moving,
That is why I'm standing still.

Now I'm hiding in the fountain,
Shivering, shining, in the rain,
Hunters creeping in upon me,
Cannot wait to cause me pain.

Now I'm leaping sudden skyward,
Flying fierce before my foes,
But the shells explode so quickly,
Never will escape their blows.

Now I'm floundering on the sidewalk,
Bleeding in the cracks below,
Now my last breath leaves my body,
Fading soft and deep and slow.

In my carcass lies the folly,
Of the lives I thought I'd save,
Broken, bleeding, too-soon leaving,
From this life I led so brave.

<u>25</u>

I Saw a Little Baby

I saw a little baby,
Who knew more than I knew,
About the living essence,
The brew he just ensued,
The teeming, moving aspect
Of a million morning suns,
A newly living, breathing,
Miraculous someone.

<u>26</u>

The Gay Wedding

I'm standing here
You're standing there
We're looking 'cross a chasm.

As we approach
The chasm deep
We see a bridge is building.

Still the distance
It is long
The future far unfolding.

Yet hope not short
And longing love
Embraces slowly changing.

We make our home
The best we can
Barriers gradually breaking.

And reaching out
We can touch
Now it's finally crumbling.

False walls that some celebrate
In the name of God
Are coming down
With passion strong
For everything ennobling.

"God is love!"
Is all we've heard
Ringing from the rafters.

So, our love
Begins anew
Grows greater ever after.

<u>27</u>

I'm Just Here to Look Good

I'm just here to look good,
I'm not here to cry,
I ain't got no feelings
balled way up inside.

I'm not like the others,
heart upon my sleeve,
sometimes even wonder
if I bleed.

Armageddon's coming,
that's what some
folks say,
just hoping that it don't
come today.

Got too much to do,
got too much to say,
if only I could find
escape some way.

Truth is not so nimble,
when your mouth is glued up tight,
and this dull expression
cannot hide my fright.

<u>28</u>

I Buy What I Want (The Miracle Man)

I buy what I want
I take what I can
I am what I am
The Miracle Man.

America loves me
China too
I'll never make
a capitalist blue.

The seas are so short
The sky so quick
I do what I must
Cuz I am so rich.

What about the dear planet?
Don't give it a thought
As a matter of fact
It's already been bought.

You say there are poor people
Can't buy a thing
I give 'em my prayers
And hope on a wing.

<u>29</u>

A Good Walking Road

A walking road, cracked,
Graveled at the shoulders,
Trees semi-arching overhead,
Old, blacktopped,
A good walking road.

Hatless, strolling,
Can't see too far ahead
Or behind for that matter.
What I've passed, I can't remember,
While my eyes strain to see
More clearly up ahead.

<u>30</u>

I Cannot

I cannot return to the table,
I cannot partake
for my own sake.

I cannot lie in the bed,
so grim,
don't let me in.

I cannot see the sweet smile
from so long ago,
just a big hole.

I cannot believe in
a love everlasting,
as I see it passing.

I cannot remember
my sin,
it's buried within.

31

He Had Lost One Arm

He had lost one arm,
The other in his pocket.
Unfortunately,
Someone had pulled it
From its socket.

<u>32</u>

I Have Breathed My Final Breath

I have breathed my final breath,
Still have not been laid to rest,
After all is done and said,
Resurrect the thief instead.

33

Here Comes That Hybrid Bus

Here comes that fancy hybrid bus.
The old bus now seems little.
This one, just to make the turns,
Bends right there in the middle.

Boy, it really looks so clean,
And so very bright.
Too bad not a single soul,
Is riding it tonight.

34

Waning Moon

A waning moon
Shimmers in the haze,
Silhouetting the trees.
I look out the lantern-lit window
To the distant mountain peaks,
Standing over the trees.
Moonlight reflects on the snow,
Making eerie light.
My heart should be filled with wonder,
Instead it lies naked,
In solemn, self-indulgence.
Pity of tears
Befriending me,
I urge them on,
Suffering, suffering,
Wallow in my misery,
Curling around me,
Crushing me in death-like dirge.
Or is it only dramatic license?

35

Unknown Unknowns

Unknown unknowns,
Aren't strolling down the street,
They're hiding in the doorways,
Where dark and light don't meet.

Seldom do they show themselves
To those who will not see.
Even less do they appear
To those who don't believe.

But if you have the greatest faith,
Unknowns become so known,
That without a single fact,
You'll never be alone.

Peace and pure contentment,
Always by your side,
Enveloped in your certainty,
Doubts will soon subside.

And thinking becomes harder,
Questioning not a cure,
Living becomes easier,
This I know for sure.

<u>36</u>

I Remember

I remember the fan at night
blowing from the window frame
seamless as a summer breeze
cooling as a rain-soaked eve.

I remember the mantra sound
whirring voiceless in the night
wrapping up like fresh cocoons
blankets bundling up just right.

I remember dreams so fine
floating on those wings of sleep
stirring up the sunlit days
all those memories so bright.

37

I Smell the Grass in the Yard

I smell the grass in the yard
Just been mowed
Smells a bit like hay
On a farm-day morn
And I'm sitting out back
As the sunlight grows
And spreads like a sheet
Across the long porch slow
And I'm dreaming now
About what might have been
And I'm wondering why
I didn't begin
All the things I thought
That I'd do
Not one of them
Ever came true.

Now my wife's home
And my children too
The day nearly over
The daily grind not through.

38

It's Only a Song

A Beatles band,
Singing of love,
Brought back memories
Like a light from above.
Everyone swaying,
Feeling so good,
Kids are all playing,
Teens act like they should.
Hugging each other,
Laughing so hard,
Everyone smiling,
In that big crowd.
But then I am startled
By the look on her face,
That boy is squealing,
As he's dragged from this place.
She must outweigh him
By 300 pounds,
Her authority showing,
As he sprawls on the ground.
"Love is all you need..."
Soars from the stage,
The message is lost,

In the midst of her rage.

We can sing all the anthems,
Hum right along,
But in the end,
It's only a song.

<u>39</u>

I Know I Love the Rain

I think I like the rain,
Pounding on the windowpane.
I enjoy that soaring sound
As it blows through trees and towns,
With children wading through
The fast appearing pools,
While cars just sit and wait,
The drops decide their fate.

I know I love the rain,
There's magic to be gained
As nature pours its soul
Wherever it may flow.

40

I Walked the Lake Today

I walked the lake today,
walked the sand,
the winter beach,
breaking in the 50's,
daylight savings kicking in,
small flows still,
washing near the shores,
waves touching melting snow.

I walked the winter beach,
in unabashed solitude,
watched a dog run;
a still-bundled child
played on nearly-dry board walks
or rested in mother's arms;
the city in the distance
looks very busy,
steam still rising from the heights,
bursting, bustling, simmering,
though so large,
seems so far,
so far from here.

41

The Cat Won't Speak to Me

The cat won't speak to me,
Though something's on his mind.
He's been staring in that mirror
A long, long time.

First, I even asked him,
Then I gave him space,
Still he won't approach me,
He follows his own pace.

Now he's moving smoothly,
From chair to couch he walks,
Now he's licking at my hand
Likely wanting just the salt.

Now he curls up in my lap
And stares into my eyes.
Sometimes words get in the way
Of love for a lifetime.

<u>42</u>

Overhearing the Biological Parents

Overhearing the biological parents,
visiting next door
with their children placed
in protective foster care.
I judge these white faces quickly for
they paint the ignorant, white trash,
hillbilly portrait perfectly.
No wonder their children were
removed for the likely-more-than
verbal abuse coming from their mouths
constantly,
the cursing, vocal outrages,
butchered grammar, yelling, even in the
presence of the caseworker.
Words exchanged between the children
mirror this world of ignorance,
of mean-spiritedness.
I shake my head.
Then a thought enters my mind.
They sound just like some of the
black families I have heard,
who I had forgiven
long ago.

<u>43</u>

If One More Girl Says No

If one more girl says no,
Says no and smiles,
Says no and is my friend,
Says no and flirts in the sexy dress
With my emotions
Roaring in the distance…

If only love were as easy as the
movies,
And we could wish it into
existence,
Or fantasize it to be,
The world would be a lot less
lonely.
But real love takes work.
If only someone would offer me a job.

<u>44</u>

If the Happiness of Others

If the happiness of others,
Could somehow blend,
And extend outside their private realms,
And touch a friend…

Then know it's been done,
Precisely by you two,
Your silliness and laughter,
Has hit me like the flu.

There have been no bad effects,
I have not taken ill,
Rather I've been lifted up,
Joy become my cure.

To watch you guys, fills me up,
So lucky to have met,
Across the oceans you have come,
So settled with yourselves.

And now, such a special day,
So much you have done,
So far you have yet to go,
Your love has just begun.

<u>45</u>

I'm Going to School Today

I'm going to school today,
I got my little bag,
I'm heading for the doorway,
My folks begin to pray.
The bullets sometimes flying,
'Cross the schoolyard,
One day one might just hit me,
This life is so, so hard.

46

My Dog is Silly

My dog is silly,
Just like you.
You see he wears
Underwear too.

He took it up,
When he was young,
But now look what
He has become.

The other dogs laugh
When he walks by.
Sometimes he'll sit
Alone and cry.

He can't change,
He's tried already,
The underwear
Keeps him steady.

Every time
He has to go,
They help him hold
Back the flow.

47

I Was a Nobody

I was a nobody
'til they found me dead,
stuffed in a dumpster
without my head.

That's about all
the headlines said.
Most of the details
were never read.

Who was I?
Where was I from?
What did I feel?
How far I'd come.

My life flew by in such a blur,
Only my death caused a stir.

My husband's grief-stricken,
that's what he'll say.
Never mention
how we fought that day.
Didn't believe him
when he said I'd pay.

I think I hit him in the face,
about that time, I left this place.

Sorrow spreads everywhere
to all the strangers gathered there,
standing in the pouring rain,
dying to glimpse my last remains.

Such a turnout at the grave.
Someone's asking, "Was she saved?"
Finally, I am set free
from all this world's hypocrisy.

48

I'm Just Here Among You

I'm just here among you,
right behind your car.
There's another one behind me,
and I don't know who they are.
The taillights string before me,
and behind me,
and beyond.
We snake to the horizon,
Just might be here 'til dawn.
We mostly sit here numbly,
Most of us alone,
Looking at our cell phones,
Even though we have a home.
Not so far away,
Not as the crow flies,
But on these endless highways,
We'll be here for some time.
There must be something better.
Perhaps electric or a train.
But then again
that won't feed
the Freedom
that we've gained.

So exhaust keeps pluming skyward,
The greenhouse gases real.
Will I keep on driving
'Til my fingers cease to feel!?

(Do you fear the Global Warming?
Is the message getting old?
Just like little children,
We won't stop until we're told.)

49

I'm Watching Young People

I'm watching young people,
Watch them on the screen,
watch them playing parts,
where I have never been.

Now they're being coy
Then they're being cute,
usually they're sardonic to boot.

They're always attractive,
quirky but sure,
ever eager to give this world a whirl.

They're kissing everybody,
everyone's their friends,
they're funny and caring and crazy,
and we all know the end.

They're walking in the sunset,
silhouette so pure,
bright melancholy I barely can endure.

50

I'm Wearing a Peace Shirt

I'm wearing a peace shirt,
I don't know what for,
I'm wearing a peace shirt,
I'm going to war.

I had to do something
With my life,
I had to do something.
To escape all this strife.

My crazy music
Didn't thrill me no more,
My friends had got lazy,
Stoned on the floor.

My boss was a loser,
Wouldn't get off my back,
Was stacking the shelves,
When I finally got sacked.

I lived with my parents,
I really got bored,
They'd did their best,
But I always was sore.

I often got angry,
Then tried to relax,
I needed some purpose,
The train left the tracks.

I'm wearing a peace shirt,
Believe that I'm good,
The government's lying,
This ain't Hollywood.

51

Indifference Remarkable

Indifference remarkable
Typical suffering
Lip curls casually
Waitress' tattoos
Welcome you
She'd rather be
Anywhere but here.

<u>52</u>

"Now I Lay Me Down to Sleep" No. 2

"Now I lay me down to sleep,
I pray the Lord my soul to keep,
If I should die before I wake,
I pray the Lord my soul to take."

Having precious children pray
Such things if they should go away?
Pray not of life and all its joys,
But pray of death and all its woes?

Even though hearts would break.
This they pray, for heaven's sake.

What kind of God
Would preach such things?
Is this the kind of love He brings?

Perhaps He wants us to live,
And give the things that Christ did give.
Like faith and hope,
And broader vision,
Like truth and love,
Not derision.

Though heaven does seem awfully grand,
I still don't quite understand.
Can eternity repay
The misery some face every day?

<u>53</u>

My Backside

The mirror reflected
in the window outside
the appearance of
my backside.
To my horror,
revealed to me,
a vision all the others see.
Whenever I turn away in pride,
lost perhaps to my backside.

54

Kill a Terrorist

Kill a terrorist
He's happy
Going to see Allah
Immediately
His offspring
Will want to kill us more.
Never going to win
That kind of war.

<u>55</u>

Liberal Guilt

Liberal guilt,
What is it for?
Liberal guilt,
The Homeless and Poor.
Liberal guilt,
Famine and War.
Don't you know
We've got to do more.
Liberal guilt,
Black vs. White,
Any injustice
Deserves the good fight.
Liberal guilt,
I wish I didn't care.
Liberal guilt,
My cross to bear.

(Liberal guilt,
Now I have become
The one that needs help.
Boy, am I stunned!)

56

Memorial Day

Memorial Day,
I missed the parade,
I missed the flag,
watching it wave.
I missed the colors,
red, white, and blue,
over the bodies
that died for you.

Young men and women,
marching there.
Soon going back,
not sure where.
They really believe
in what they do,
defending democracy
for me and you.

Perhaps one day
I'll hear their names
on the nightly news,
hope no one is blamed.

I pray for them
now and then,
I pray for peace,
again and again,
I pray against
these senseless wars,
just as I did
years before.

57

Racism in the Bar

WHITE GUY #1:
_____ had a good game.
 (black guy)
Course, he's not there to think.
That's why they need _____ in there.
                            (white guy)

WHITE GUY #2: Yeah, nods.

WHITE GUY #1:
To stop that street ball they play,
You know what I mean?

WHITE GUY #2: Yeah, nods.

WHITE GUY #1:
Sure can jump and jam, though.
But you know in college,
They don't go to classes,
Just there to play ball.

Others take the classes for them.
Or it's all phys. ed.
Or wood working.
You know what I mean?

WHITE GUY #2: Yeah.

WHITE GUY #1:
But they sure can play ball,
can't they?

WHITE MAN #2: Yeah, nods.

I, WHITE MAN #3, wince, but don't say a
thing…

Again.

<u>58</u>

I Will Kill That Thing

I will kill that thing
inside of me.
Your voice,
labeling me this, that,
the other,
that I never was
but you almost created.
I will crush with the
heel of my boot
the hate that seeped
into my bones,
encouraged by you.
I will smash with
a mighty rock
the walking lies
that sounded like the
the truth,
to the untrained ear,
as they emerged
from your monstrous mouth.

59

Put Me in a Room

Put me in a room,
And now you make me wait,
Staring at diplomas
While my dinner's getting late.

Why didn't I bring that magazine,
Or a book or two?
At least I could then pass the time,
Perhaps learn something new.

Right there, there is a mini skull.
There's a bony hand.
Right up there, a diagram
Of a full-sized man!

I hope that he will hurry.
I wonder if he'll knock.
I don't know what to think of him.
I just know he's a doc.

60

Sagging Porch

She knew what she should do
with the past,
Yet stood upon the sagging porch
And saddled up that muddled memory
That haunted her as she rode
Over former hills of green
Now burned and gray
with regret.

61

See the Young Teens

See the young teens
walking
Fresh in youthful
glow
You quickly know the status
By the girls that lead the
show
Ranking at the bottom
Are the last ones in the
row.

62

Seemed a Time That Was Blessed

Seemed a time that was blessed,
As we rushed past today.
Had no time to rest,
We were carried away.
And we raised up our hands,
Like the newly enslaved.
And marched to the bands,
Though there was no parade.
And we took all our meaning,
Thought we felt deep within,
And gave it away to ordinary men.
The ads gained their focus,
A style bought and sold,
Discovered the hippie
Was made out of gold.

<u>63</u>

She's All Grown Up

She's all grown up,
exclaiming, "I laughed so hard at work,
I fell out of my chair!"
Roaring heartily, smiling broadly,
"I have a boyfriend!"
Loudly, delightedly.

She's not okay,
some say,
her parents silent to her
enthusiasms.
Others just don't
burst forth,
some say,
with such
odd abandon.
Father firmly admonishes,
"Be careful with those boys,
<u>be careful!</u>"

(they might love you as you are).

64

Talk, Talk

Talk, talk
raging talk
hurts my head
I start to walk
but then I stop
by what's been said
the very best
is in your head
what you think
then what you say
makes for me
a splendid day
I don't believe
that I could sleep
if I didn't hear
your words so deep
they engage my mind so
there's nothing else
I need to know
talk, talk
it pleases you
but for me
it's nothing new.

<u>65</u>

That Amazing Body

That amazing body
is able to do
the most incredible
things,
flying down the court,
behind the back,
the ball is passed,
soaring
in flight,
the ball caught,
and flipped
from fingertips,
swishing musically
through the
distant net.

That amazing body
can fling
that ball
a football field,
perfectly into
the extended arms
of an equally amazing receiver,
racing headlong

to pull that ball
into muscled chest,
while simultaneously
hammered by a
multitude of equally
amazing defenders,
in efforts
to jar that ball
loose,
yet already strongly nestled
in firm but cradle-like
grasp.

That amazing body,
peering at the pitcher,
bat poised,
successfully hitting
a 98-mph ball,
now sailing off the bat,
soaring 400 ft.
over the head
of the equaling amazing outfielder,
rushing headlong,
glove outstretched,
slamming forcefully into the wall,
withstanding the impact,
crashing to the ground,
sprawled on the grass,

dazedly raising his arm,
revealing the ball,
somehow secured safely in his grasp.

With spectators cheering,
and millions paid,
but with equally amazing minds;

that may cheat, and lie,
ingest drugs foolishly,
overly arm themselves needlessly,
steal, and gamble recklessly,
beat a girlfriend/wife
purposely,
train dogs to fight
for sport and pleasure;

oblivious to right and wrong,
normal moral imperatives
lost in the crowd's
roaring accolades.

66

I Watched the Band Carefully

I watched the band carefully
As though I can play.
Examined their fingers
To show me the way.
Their licks are quite moving,
Stroking the neck.
My confidence lagging,
I sit down to rest.
All this performing
Is taking its toll.
Pretending this lifestyle
Is making me old.

67

The Little Girls

The little girls,
Pretend ballerinas
In their tights
And feathery skirts,
Beginning to be coached
Toward the feminine
Before they know it.
Few boys in tights
By their sides,
Rather outside
With football helmets
And hardware.

68

You Boys Used to Lie on the Ground

"You boys used to lie on the ground
and watch the storm clouds roll in,"
mom remembered.
And so did I,
with dawning smile.

The ground to my back
still feels solid, steady,
The force of gravity
seems to pull the spine
properly in place,
arms and legs akimbo,
now angel-like,
makes me more fully
flatten into the earth.

The sky overhead is maddening,
clouds drifting (shifting) darkly
beneath the mass,
wisps breaking free,
floating rapidly away as if making for another
dimension.

In the far west
rays of light cut across the sky, Jesus-like,
descending in sharp, straight, or alternating,
angular lines,
beacons breaking through cloud cracks,
beautifully bathing the earth,
the wind rises, pushing heavy clouds above
the land,
casting huge shadows across the fields,
moving in patches,
obliterating then revealing the landscape in
light.

Downpours in the distance
show as impenetrable, dark-hued bands,
extending from the lower half of mountainous,
cloud banks.
The wind picks up further as the display
approaches
and cold, scattered droplets now splash on our
skin,
refreshing after a warm day,
but growing uncomfortable as they come more
heavily.

Thunder cracks and occasionally lightning
darts down from the sky,
briefly revealing a crisp,

illuminated countryside.
We actually hope to see funnel clouds
curling down.
Sometimes we chase the storms
clumsily across picked cornfields,
corn stubble grabbing at our feet.

There was nothing larger,
nothing so diminishing,
nothing as beautiful.
Storms crossed the prairie
like gladiators,
fought their battles,
and left us awed and always more alive
in their wake.

69

The Moon Shone Like a Silver Plate

The moon shone like a silver plate
hanging overhead.
The taillights ahead of me
held more than just my friend.
The road stretched to the horizon,
like it had before.
The night beckoned brightly,
and I was feeling sure,
about this road I'm traveling,
the distance up ahead,
the place that I am going,
this life I've so far led.

70

The News Was Dismal

The news was dismal,
as usual,
only bad news sells,
you know.

All deaths were top
of the news line;
from accidents, murders,
and wars.

Many of those
were so hideous,
I couldn't stop wondering,
What for?

From innocent crossfire slayings,
To barrel bombing the suffering and poor.

I don't know why
I keep listening.
It's only bringing me down.
Each time I hear
of a life gone out,

It makes an emptying sound.
An ache I cannot extinguish,
tears a hole in my heart,
mounting a terrible mourning,
that feels like it never will stop.

With every life that is stolen,
Part of our essence takes leave,
Scatters in space with the memory,
Quietly starts to recede.

Then I feel the touch of my children,
Loving and warm as can be,
Laughing while hugging me fiercely,
Reviving my need to believe.

71

There's a BMW

There's a BMW
in his office.
There's a laser
on his ring.
There's a model
of a hand right there,
and he'll be cutting.

He mostly deals in surgery
of the cosmetic kind.
I hope he can
just fix my hand.
I've had an awful time.

He won't be fixing
up my nose,
or give a tummy-tuck.
He won't be hampering
my prose,
or change what I
think up.

I just want
a better hand
to hug the folks
I like.
I don't want a
better brand,
or a different life.

<u>72</u>

The Sun Shone

The sun shone
on me today
I opened up
like a flower
too long dead
took in the rays
like a grateful flag
unfurled
over
all
the empty graves
the wars
gave up trying to
fill
as peace
finally ruled
the world.

73

The Chicago Homeless Monitors

Have you ever heard of the Chicago Bird
Collision Monitors (CBCM)?

Birds, especially during migration time,
slam into city skyscrapers
that weren't there for their ancestors;
well-lit high-rises act
like a beacon to their flight;
that abrupt halting
spills them onto the streets below,
stunned,
to be devoured by dogs or cats,
crushed by the large instep
of a careless commuter, or simply suffer street
life in other sundry ways.

Volunteers journey downtown at 5:00 a.m.,
and rescue these victims of our
expansive civilization.
Some birds, though seemingly lifeless,
are still with us
and only need nurturing hands
to gather them up
and lend them time,
time to gather their wits and senses.

After transport,
careful examination,
and treatment as needed,
they may continue on their journey.

This is so humane, this cause,
this group of volunteers.

Have you ever heard of the Chicago Homeless
Monitors?
Neither have I.

<u>74</u>

The Urban Boisterous Boy

The urban, boisterous boy
Was attempting to climb
The slippery lamppost,
In lieu of trees.

<u>75</u>

I'm Digging Out the Coal

I'm digging out the coal
Sometimes it pays real good
I don't pity the mine
The mine pities me.

There's no other job around
Except this torturing the land
The black dust in my mouth
The black dust in the sky.

The paycheck in her hands
Travels to the kids' mouths
They chew themselves green in the face
Thank God they have something to chew.

The choices are thin
Line the exposed earth
The boss tips his hat
The gears continue to grind.

The grinding gets the job done
The northern clean kitchen hums
The curly fluorescent light bulbs
Screwed tight will last forever.

The coal won't last that long
The clean coal will come
Even the clean coal will be used up
We return to oil.

76

A New Soft Wind

Tonight, I feel a new, soft wind,
Rattling my blinds again,
Rising up from this nice night,
Cold storm clouds moved out of sight,
Leaving breath from spring's fresh air,
To brush my senses lying here,
Taking in this gift we're given,
Whether from nature or from heaven.
Enjoy it now to the fullest
Before the routine returns to dull us.

77

There's an Old Man

There's an old man
In a chair
Over there,
Across the busy street.
He's got a pennant behind,
So that he can be seen.

He's sitting so quietly,
He could be asleep,
He's facing the restaurant,
While everyone eats.

His motorized chair is resting,
As he seems to be,
The silence is deafening,
Beneath that tree,
He's sitting alone,
One day you or me.

<u>78</u>

There's Another Condo

There's another condo
Growing on this block
Disappearing architecture
Once a perfect spot.

And the proud traditions
History and art
Bled into the neighborhood
Enlivening our lot.

But now I see the strangers
Often come in twos
Pockets full of money
Sameness in their shoes.

<u>79</u>

There's Something Coming from Your Ear

There's something coming from your ear.
It makes me scared at first.
You seem to be oblivious
To what could be the worst
Disease that we have ever seen,
I pray that you will live.
Then I see you talking,
But no one's really there.
Now you're singing loudly
As though you do not hear.
And when I talk to you,
You ignore me so,
It makes me feel invisible,
Or just a great, big bore.
Until you sweetly tell me,
It's just your blue-tooth® phone,
And your loud, loud music
That makes me feel alone.
Then suddenly I remember
What Darwin had to say,
Survival of the fittest
Could do you in one day.
Just then I hear a truck
Careening up the curb.

I leap just in time,
But you are dead for sure.

80

Time is Far Away

Time is far away,
and 'round the corner,
hovering,
not foretelling the future,
waiting for no one,
least of all me.

Time is at once beckoning,
a life of being better
or worse,
not knowing.

Time is not revealed,
no one's friend,
no one's enemy,
neutral,
there to become
whatever we make it,
but only after it arrives.

Some say,
Some say,
it is written,
success, failure,

life, death,
unchanged,
no matter what we do,

The iceberg mostly hidden,
floating in the darkness.

81

Victim of Youth Culture

Victim of youth culture,
That's what they said,
And the mirror can't lie,
Like the thoughts in your head.

You ache when you move,
But you say you're not old,
Yet even in summer,
You always feel cold.

You still enjoy watching
The latest of crazes,
You try to join in,
But screw up the cool phrases.

When you talk to your children,
You want to seem hip,
But they mostly ignore you,
And give you some lip.

You wear the new fashions
But you shouldn't even try
Despite all your effort,
Your body can't lie.

You wonder what happened.
The years went so fast,
You just are not ready,
To give up your past.

82

Wondering

Wondering
about
the bigger things,
Wandering
about
in endless rings,
Circling
the parallel drive,
Always,
Always,
feeling alive,
Despite the tearing emotion,
Rolling with the constant motion,
Never,
Never,
standing still,
Moving even against my will,
Searching, such an old cliché,
Becoming, my virtual slave,
Never can be what it isn't,
Declare that it is omnipresent,
Shakes me to the very depths,
Never giving rise to rest.

83

You Have All the Money

You have all the money
The good things in life
The family and friendships
Without sacrifice.

Can't you see others
Living without.
They deserve something better
Then living in doubt.

We could raise up your taxes
You then could do more
Then hiding your billions
Somewhere offshore.

Redistribute your money
To the needy and poor
Investing the future
In people, not war.

Then they could gain
The things that you have
All would help others
All would be glad.

Equality would flourish
We'd all be the same
Nothing to strive for
No one left to blame.

84

Modern Wife

There is a wife
In a very short dress,
Taut, thin top
Enhances her breasts,
High heels accent
Her aching limbs,
Proudly walking
Next to him.

A body for longing you can't deny,
Little boy strolling by her side,
Hand hooked in the belt loop of her man,
Everyone staring would understand,
She's not available for caresses,
June Cleaver's image
Lost in her successes.

<u>85</u>

Hello There, People

Hello there, people, in the sky,
Mars your destination?
Why not have some apple pie
From the United Nations?

America, I can't see you,
Hardly see the earth.
Up above the endless stars,
Welcomed our world's birth.

Sun sure is bright here,
Blinding you might say,
Everything God giveth,
He just might take away.

They said that we must colonize,
Earth's become so ruined,
Had to find another home,
My life's just not worth losing.

So far Mars seems quite nice,
Just some old erosion,
But tough to make good atmosphere
With nuclear explosions.

Before the land was barren,
But now they say it's molten,
A barbecue would fit right in,
A pit just can't be chosen.

Now I have my condo,
And cases of "New Coke®."
Stroll out on my breezeway,
Hear my brand-new joke:

Two astronauts were skating,
But one fell through the ice,
The other kept on going,
And "called it paradise."

<u>86</u>

I'd Like to Be a Housewife

"I'd like to be a housewife,"
Someone heard her say,
"I know that I could clean real good,
Hope babies come my way."

"I'd like to be a housewife,
Meet my husband's every whim,
I know I could make him feel
Just like a king."

"I'd like to be a housewife,
Join the PTA,
Bring cakes and cookies to events,
Of course, the people pay."

"So, you'd like to be a housewife,"
The trafficker did say,
"I got a good man lives right here.
He's in the USA."

<u>87</u>

Breathe in the Air

Breathe in the air,
Deeply,
Now imagine,
Within the air you breathe,
There are tiny particles
Of plastic,
Imagine how that would feel,
Imagine what that would do to your body,
To your children's bodies,
To your children's, children's bodies.

Now imagine yourself a sea turtle,
Swimming through that air,
Though it's water.
It's our beautiful
Blue, blue ocean.
And tiny pieces of plastic
Are flowing through him/her.
But unfortunately,
You don't have to imagine this.
IF you ARE a sea turtle,
You ARE sucking in plastic particles,

And absorbing them,
And absorbing them,
And absorbing them.

Now imagine sea turtles,
And us,
And the oceans,
Plastic free.

Imagination without action
Is an empty promise,
Floating on an irreparable sea.

88

Little Library Pencils

Little library pencils
Having no erasers
I wonder just who makes them
I bet someone from Asia.

Or do they just cut one up
Of the normal size
Give the erasers to the poor
To begin anew their lives.

<u>89</u>

The Flowers Are Yet to Blossom

The flowers are yet to blossom
The winter lingers still
Planted where they're not forgotten
Sunlight whispers here.

The snows are melting slowly
The earth still too cold
The blossoms therefore waiting
The warmth is coming soon.

90

Tears Wash This Soul So Clean

Tears wash this soul so clean
Wash it with a mountain stream
Flowing over rocks and sand
Traveling to some distant land
Stopping somewhere in between
This earthly life and heaven's dream.

91

The Pleasure Dome

The Pleasure Dome
Rules America,
Sweeping over our heads,
The pleasure principle.

Unjust, just?
Roll the dice.
If I want...
THINGS!
I should have them.

There are no moral decisions in the purchase,
Or the ads that drove me to it.

Into my heart the lies of
Happiness,
Belongingness,
Seep.
Surprised...
On haunches!?
Quivering...

I've seen those big eyes before.
That ad for the lost puppies
of new york.

not the lost people of Syria.

92

OBAMA   CHICAGO   2008

On that day
Everyone was black
And everyone was white
And everyone was equal
In His sight.

93

Maybe Mayberry

These times pass,
Not patiently,
Urgently,
They know what's up,
That motion,
That curled lip,
That insensitivity,
Grandstanding
For self.
You should huddle
In despair,
Kneel,
There is nothing for you here,
That life was lived,
Some sort of conscious honor
In the air,
Now gone.
I ramble,
And swear,
And emit platitudes,
Infectious,
Not me,
But I feel it,
Like coarse sand on my skin,

On my tongue,
With remorse,
What have we come to?
After a light seeming bright,
Endless,
Hope,
A myriad of mystery,
Now swollen,
Greed inflated.
Christ!
Should have seen it coming
And hidden my innocence
In that old TV show.
Which one?
So many,
Maybe Mayberry,
Maybe "Mayberry RFD."

94

I Knelt Today at the Football Game

I knelt today at the football game,
And I don't even play.
It wasn't during the anthem
Or while the player's played.
It was within the stadium,
Semi-dark hallway.
I thought the place proper,
No visual display.

I asked some simple questions,
Will He/She/It intrude
To move the people once again
To insist on being heard
And speak out against those things
That don't feel just inside,
Uphold that noble trust to reason:
What's good?
What's truth?
What's right?

<u>95</u>

The Confirmation

One side spoke first kindly,
Mirror image keen,
The other drove the doubting,
Her story stole the scene.

She was so convincing,
Carefully, she explained.
Her words now frozen on the mike,
Truth met with such disdain.

Nervous, he was speaking
This his final test
His words he now was mouthing
There's nothing to confess.

He never said I'm sorry,
Only he didn't do it,
Words came falling from his mouth,
Troubled, I saw through it.

I saw his indignation,
No one said he lied,
No one had confronted him,
Nearly all his life.

Now he sat there loudly,
Facing mostly peers,
Gentlemen of stature,
Looking so sincere.

Can't you see I'm stalwart,
Can't you see my pain,
Can't you see my pouting self,
Standing in the rain?

96

A Future Legislative Law

Now that we have
a majority of women in both
the Senate and House,
have you heard of the
new abortion law?

Any man found guilty,
through extensive DNA research,
of siring an aborted fetus,
will spend a minimum
of 90 years in federal prison.

97

Chase the Demon

Chase the demon,
Chase the demon,
At your back door,
In your back pocket.

Chase the demon,
Chase the demon,
Breathe the air,
Exhale slowly in remembrance.

Chase the demon,
Chase the demon,
Chewing on black muscle,
Chewing and chewing.

Chase the demon,
Chase the demon,
Chiseled gun in his mouth,
Drooling only excess

Chase the demon
Chase the demon,
Salivating green, green, green
Piles of sordid cash.

Chase the demon,
Chase the demon,
Striving woman in his mouth,
Gasping, gasping, gasping.

Chase the demon,
Chase the demon,
Swallowing your pre-existing condition
whole,
Then spitting it back.

Chase the demon,
Chase the demon,
Evangelicals doze,
Betrayed by a Judas' kiss.

Chase the demon,
Chase the demon,
Fooled workingmen, prone,
Devoured by Wall Street.

Chase the demon,
Chase the demon,
Withering war rhetoric
Spilling from his careless mouth.

Chase the demon,
Chase the demon,
Quashing courage,
Replacing it with toadyism.

Chase the demon,
Chase the demon,
Neo-Nazi on his arm,
Reminiscing.

Chase the demon,
Chase the demon,
Roughly pushing past our friends,
Embracing his tyrants.

Chase the demon,
Chase the demon,
Democracy's honored voice
Now 'enemy of the people.'

Chase the demon,
Chase the demon,
LIES, bouncing like a lottery ball,
Not a one has landed.

Chase the demon,
Chase the demon,
Tweeting a tsunami,
Name-calling nearly an entire nation.

Chase the demon,
Chase the demon,
Banning Muslims,
But not the KKK.

Chase the demon,
Chase the demon,
Murdered journalist's parts,
Scattered in the wake.

Case the demon,
Chase the demon,
Immigrant arm extended,
Now her child is dead.

Chase the demon,
Chase the demon,
Encouraging the divide,
Then toasting its blood.

Chase the demon,
Chase the demon,
Heating up the hatred,
And happily holding an unlit match.

Chase the demon,
Chase the demon,
Loud, twisted, braggadocio,
Echoing, echoing, echoing.

Chase the demon,
Chase the demon,
Come to perch on the back
Of modern chaos.
And loving it!

Chase the demon,
Chase the demon,
Until he stops,
Until he stops,
Until he finally stops.

98

My Mind Is Blank.

My mind is blank,
Nothing to say,
No thoughts meandering,
No meaningless melancholy,
No irony,
No absurdity,
No social commentary,
No emotion,
No action,
My mind is blank,
Resting from overuse.
No inspiration,
No observations,
Just hesitation,
Lost imagination,
No failed relations,
No predictions,
Or depressions,
My mind is blank.
Can't contemplate,
A clean slate,
A fresh break,
My mind is blank.

99

Happiness

Laughing once
I remember
Tearing
My world asunder
Quick to chuckle
See the humor
Irony will soon deliver
Me from all those low times
Absurdities
Make endless rhymes
Of life's colossal situations
Create internal observations
Watch me giggle
Soon to grin
Got to be the origins
Of the seeing and believing
Happiness my new religion.

100

To This Blessing I Will Come (Mom's Passing)

To this blessing I will come,
Earthly wishes, they will end,
Future bright, unending, true,
Bathed in light, all things new,
Welcome me in glistening robes,
Love engulfs me as I go.

Bonus Poem

A New Kind of Love

May the years bring a new kind of love,
A love there is always more of.
Our past or present can't take away,
This love in us is fierce each day.
To shore us up when things are wrong,
Much softer than just being strong.
A love that acts,
That may not talk,
That lives and breathes,
And walks the walk.
That blossoms when confronted,
Yet never discounts the other.
A love that's open,
Does not judge,
A love that is,
The best of us.
A love that's neither right nor wrong,
A love just there,
Need not be found,
To tap into when things are tough,

And never can be too much.
Just there and ready,
Pouring forth,
A power, presence, a force for hope.

WORKS CITED

1. "I Remember How He Prayed" p.1
The Holy Bible Revised Standard Version
Containing the Old and New Testaments.
Thomas Nelson and Sons, Toronto, New York,
Edinburgh. (1952). My note to reader: Matt.
5:9 constitutes the first half of this quote, Matt.
5:5 the second half.

2. "A Picture's Worth a Thousand Words" p.3
English Idiom. WIKIPEDIA:
*Speakers Give Sound Advice". Syracuse Post-
Dispatch. page 18. March 28, 1911.*
*"One Look Is Worth A Thousand Words".Piqua
Leader-Dispatch.. page 2. August 15, 1913.*
*"Pictorial Magazine of the War
(advertisement)". San Antonio Light. page 6.
January 10, 1918.The Dictionary of Clichés* by
James Rogers (Ballantine Books, New York,
1985)

38. "It's Only a Song" p.46
Lennon, John and Paul McCartney. "Love is all
you need.." <u>All You Need is Love</u>. Magical
Mystery Tour. CD. EMI Records Ltd. (1967).

52. "Now I Lay Me Down to Sleep No. 2" p.64
WIKIPEDIA: *The New England Primer,* 1750
ed., p. 28.

73. "Chicago Homeless Monitors" p.94
Chicago Bird Collision Monitors (CBCM),
from their website (www.birdmonitors.net):
a volunteer conservation project dedicated to
the protection of migratory birds through
rescue, advocacy and outreach." For further
information, see website.

84. "Modern Wife" p.111
June Cleaver, character on TV show, "Leave It
to Beaver." Created by Joe Connelly and Bob
Mosher. CBS. (1957-1963).

85. "Hello There, People" p.112
Henley, Don and Glenn Frey. "Call something
[it] paradise…" The Last Resort. Hotel
California. CD. Electra/Asylum/Nonesuch
Records. (1976).

91. "The Pleasure Done" p.120
WICKIPEDIA: In Freudian psychoanalysis,
the **pleasure principle** (German:
Lustprinzip)[1] is the instinctive seeking
of pleasure and avoiding of pain to satisfy
biological and psychological needs.[2]
 Specifically, the pleasure principle is the
driving force guiding the id.[3]
1.Laplanche, Jean; Pontalis, Jean-
Bertrand (1988) [1973]. "Pleasure Principle (pp.
322-5)". The Language of Psycho-
analysis (reprint, revised ed.). London: Karnac

Books. ISBN 978-0-946-43949-2. ISBN 0-94643949-4.
2.*Snyder, C. R.; Lopez, Shane J. (2007). Positive Psychology. Sage Publications, Inc. p. 147. ISBN 0-7619-2633-X.*
3.*Carlson, Neil R.; Heth, C. Donald (2007). Psychology - the science of behaviour. Pearson Education Canada. p. 700. ISBN 978-0-205-64524-4.*

93. "Maybe Mayberry" p.123
Mayberry, fictional town featured on the TV shows: "Andy Griffith Show." Created by Sheldon Leonard. CBS. (1960-1968); and "Mayberry RFD" (see below).
"Mayberry RFD". TV show. Created by Bob Ross. CBS. (1968-1971).

Back Cover: "The Grass Is Always Greener on the Other Side of the Fence." WIKIPEDIA: The renowned Oxford Dictionary of English Proverbs (1970) does not even have a separate entry for the proverb, "The grass is always greener on the other side of the fence." Instead it lists the Latin proverb, "Fertilior seges est alieno semper in arvo," cited by Erasmus of Rotterdam which was published in English translation by Richard Taverner in 1545 as "The corne in an other mans ground semeth euer more fertyll and plentifull then doth oure owne."

ACKNOWLEDGEMENTS

To John Lambert and Rick Leddy for their
constant and ongoing friendship, reading,
suggestions, inspiration, and support; to Bruce
Hirsch and Bill Nemchok for providing/
suggesting some of the soundtrack to my life; to
my sons Ian and Eric for their love and
continuous inspiration and support; to my mom
and dad, Harvey and Sue Jackson, especially for
the core values they gave me; to my brothers
and sisters (and brothers and sisters-in-laws),
Kathy and Bill Jackson-Miller, Nan and Lee
Bucksten, Charles and Beth Jackson, Gary and
Pat Jackson, Tom and Lisa Jackson, and Russ
and Jane Jackson, and their families, who have
always been there for me whenever needed; to
Leila Mowers (and her banjo) and Christine
Jackson-Cercowy, (especially to Chris for co-
producing our amazing children) and their
families, for sharing some of my journey; to
Ruth Kunc, Robin Migalla, and Christine Pardee
for reading and commenting on my poems; to
Gareth Sitz' inspirational "Poetry Alive!" poetry
writing group, meeting monthly in Elgin, IL, at
Gail Borden Public Library; to all the
knowledgeable folks at the fantastic five-star
Elmhurst Public Library, Elmhurst, IL:
especially Kim Calkins and Susan Nunamaker
for running the Elmhurst Public Library Book

Fair, from which this book arose; Margie Kollbocker, Anne Swanson, and Bryan Blank; and the amazing library tech support crew: Jeremy, Paul, Andrew, Meredith, Amanda, and Mary (you know who you are), without whom this book would not have happened; and a big thank you to Publisher's Graphics®, Carol Stream, IL, for all their wonderful advice and work, with a special thank you to Astari Bustos for all his help; and finally to my H.S. teacher, Al Harland, who first taught me the impact and possibilities writing can have.

About the author:
Ken G. Jackson grew up in Illinois, where he still resides, living in the Chicago area. He has been writing poetry since he was a teenager. This is his first published poetry collection.

For more information: gjaxnek@gmail.com

Cover and back photo sources respectively: Elmira Grade School, Toulon, IL; photographer unknown, school picture of Ken, 1959-1960. Unknown newspaper, possibly the Kewanee Star Courier but unconfirmed, Toulon, IL and area, photographer unknown, July 17, 1953.

For those curious, the full caption at the bottom of the back-page photo reads "ELMIRA CONTESTANTS---An Elmira family is among the contestants entered in the Typical Farm Family contest. The family of Mr. and Mrs. Harvey Jackson are (left to right, front): Kathy, nine; Nan, eight; Gary, five; Tommy, three; Charles, six; (back row, left to right): Jackson, holding two-year-old Kenny, and Mrs. Jackson." (*Russ had not yet made an appearance.*)